W9-CLA-381

# THE SUN

BY ARNOLD RINGSTAD

Published by The Child's World®
1980 Lookout Drive • Mankato, MN 56003-1705
800-599-READ • www.childsworld.com

Photographs ©: GSFC/Goddard/NASA, cover,
1, 3, 8, 13, 14, 16; SSC/NASA, 2, 20, 21; Deborah
Kolb/Shutterstock Images, 4; Sergey Nivens/
Shutterstock Images, 7; Cherdchai Charasri/
Shutterstock Images, 9 (basketball); Lucie
Lang/Shutterstock Images, 9 (pin); Waraporn
Wattanakul/Shutterstock Images, 10; Ugi-Creative/
Shutterstock Images, 17; Red Line Editorial,
18 (foreground); Shutterstock Images, 18
(background); Glenn Benson/KSC/NASA, 22

Copyright © 2021 by The Child's World®
All rights reserved. No part of this book
may be reproduced or utilized in any
form or by any means without written
permission from the publisher.

ISBN 9781503844728 (Reinforced Library Binding)
ISBN 9781503846197 (Portable Document Format)
ISBN 9781503847385 (Online Multi-user eBook)
LCCN 2019958000

Printed in the United States of America

**About the Author**
Arnold Ringstad loves reading
about space science and
exploration. He lives in Minnesota
with his wife and their cat.

# CONTENTS

# CHAPTER ONE

# LIGHT FOR THE SOLAR SYSTEM

The sun shines brightly in the daytime sky. People lie on beaches in the sunlight. The light helps plants grow. The sun's heat creates wind and weather. It keeps Earth warm enough for us to survive. But what exactly is the sun?

The sun is a star. There are billions of stars in the universe. Many are larger than our sun. But our sun is still the largest object near Earth. It makes up about 99.8 percent of all the **mass** in the **solar system**. It would take more than one million Earths to fill up the sun.

◄ Life on Earth would be impossible without the sun's light and warmth.

The sun is so large that everything else in the solar system **orbits** it. That includes planets and their moons. It also includes smaller objects, such as asteroids and comets.

Like all stars, the sun is a huge ball of hot, glowing gas. The sun gives off light in all directions. When the sun's light hits a planet, some of the light turns to heat. This is how the sun warms up the objects around it.

**DID YOU KNOW?**

Light travels very fast. But the sun is about 93 million miles (150 million km) away. Light from the sun takes about eight minutes to reach Earth.

The sun is at the center of our solar system. All objects in the solar system orbit it.

# How Big Is the Sun?

Sun                                              Earth

# Basketball

## Quilting Pin

The sun is 109.2 times larger than Earth! If the sun were the size of a basketball, Earth would be the size of a quilting pin head.

# CHAPTER TWO

# INSIDE THE SUN

The sun is mostly made up of two gases. These gases are hydrogen and helium. The sun's size holds these gases together. At the sun's center, **atoms** of hydrogen and helium are squeezed tightly together. They get very hot. The temperature in the center is around 27 million degrees Fahrenheit (15 million °C).

This high temperature makes a process called **fusion** possible. Two atoms of hydrogen smash together. They combine to form one atom of helium. When they combine, they release energy. Fusion is happening all the time in the sun's center. The sun is slowly turning its hydrogen into helium.

◄ Helium is the gas that causes party balloons to float. Helium and hydrogen are the two main gases that make up the sun.

The energy from fusion does not leave the sun right away. It bounces around in the sun's thick, glowing gases. It takes around 170,000 years to reach the sun's surface. Here, the temperature is down to about 10,000 degrees Fahrenheit (5,500°C). The energy finally leaves the sun as sunlight. It spreads outward through the solar system.

**DID YOU KNOW?**

Above the sun's surface are more gases. They form the sun's **atmosphere**. The temperature here is higher than on the surface. Scientists aren't sure why this is.

The sun has an atmosphere, just like Earth does. ▶

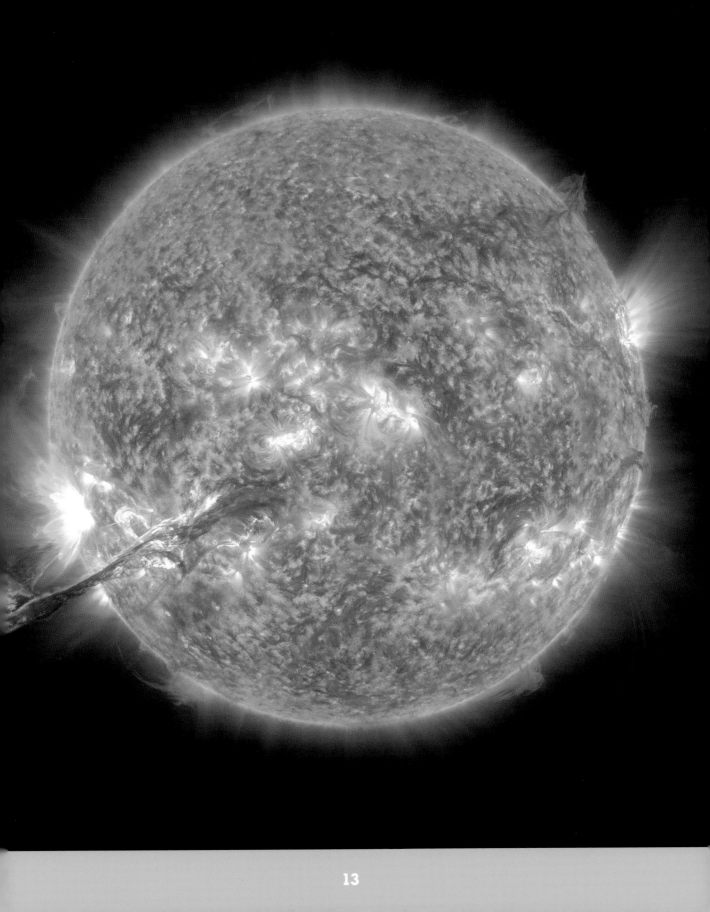

**SUNSPOT**

Sunspots are visible with special cameras.

# CHAPTER THREE

# SPACE WEATHER

The sun is an active object. Huge flames leap off its surface. Sometimes that material flies off into space. These are examples of space weather. Space weather affects the sun and the planets around it.

Sunspots are dark areas on the sun. They are caused by the sun's **magnetic field**. The magnetic field gets stronger in some areas. These areas become cooler and darker than the rest of the sun. They are called sunspots.

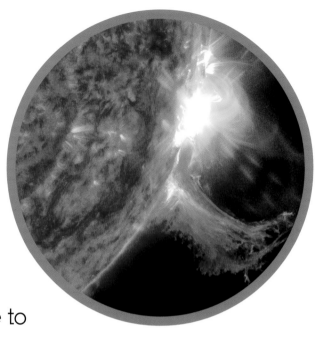

◀ Solar flares have enough energy to damage satellites.

The sun's magnetic field can also throw material off the surface. This is called a solar flare. Solar flares have a similar cause to sunspots. This means they often happen around the same time. During a solar flare, the material falls back to the sun's surface. But energy still shoots out into space. This energy reaches Earth. Our atmosphere protects us on the surface. But the energy can damage **satellites**. It could even hurt people traveling in space.

**DID YOU KNOW?**

The energy from solar flares hits Earth's magnetic field. This creates glowing lights in the night sky called auroras.

Sometimes, the sun's magnetic field throws material away so fast that it flies into space. This is called a coronal mass ejection (CME). Up to 220 billion pounds (100 billion kg) of hot gases go flying. This material zooms at 7 million miles per hour (11.3 million km/h). Most CMEs do not point toward Earth. When they do, they can harm electric devices, even on the planet's surface.

# CHAPTER FOUR

# STUDYING THE SUN

Scientists want to learn more about the sun. They study space weather. Knowing more about space weather can help protect satellites in space and electric devices on Earth. But studying the sun must be done carefully. People must never look directly at the sun. It will damage their eyes. Even sunglasses will not protect them. Luckily, scientists have found ways to safely study the sun.

One simple way to look at the sun is to poke a small hole in a sheet of thick paper. Hold the paper so it faces the sun. Then hold a second sheet a few feet behind it. You will be able to see a small image of the sun on the second sheet.

◀ Looking straight at the sun can be extremely dangerous. There are many ways to safely look at the sun, such as with solar viewers like this one.

Special telescopes can give people a closer view of the sun. It is important to never look at the sun through a regular telescope. But special telescopes have filters. The filters block most of the sun's light. They let people look at the sun closely. Sunspots and solar flares are visible.

NASA employee Leslie Lowes looks at the sun through a special solar telescope. Using a regular telescope to look at the sun is not safe.
▼

▲
People can use
safety equipment
such as solar safety
glasses to look at the sun.

The best way to study the sun is to go to
space. Scientists have launched **probes** to
learn more about the sun. The probes can get a
better view than telescopes on Earth. They can
take close-up pictures. They can learn about
space weather. Some can even fly into the sun's
atmosphere. These probes are teaching us more
than ever before about the star that makes life
on Earth possible.

# PARKER SOLAR PROBE

One mission to the sun is the *Parker Solar Probe*. This spacecraft launched from Earth in 2018. It will fly very close to the sun. Earth is about 93 million miles (150 million km) from the sun. *Parker Solar Probe* will get within 4 million miles (6.4 million km) of the sun's surface. This will bring it into the top of the sun's atmosphere.

Flying that close to the sun is hard. The heat is intense. *Parker Solar Probe* has a 4.5-inch- (11.4-cm-) thick heat shield on the side facing the sun. The shield is made out of tough material that can survive the heat. It protects the probe's cameras and scientific tools.

Getting close to a large object, such as the sun, means picking up a lot of speed. When it is closest to the sun, *Parker Solar Probe* will be going 125 miles per second (201 km/s)! At that speed, someone could fly from California to New York in about 20 seconds.

▲ In this photo, scientists test the *Parker Solar Probe* in Florida. The probe was launched in 2018.

# GLOSSARY

**atmosphere** (AT-muss-feer) An atmosphere is the layer of gases that surrounds a planet or star. The sun has a hot atmosphere.

**atoms** (AT-umz) Atoms are the smallest pieces of elements. The sun contains atoms of hydrogen and helium.

**fusion** (FEW-zhun) Fusion is the process of two atoms combining to form one atom. Two atoms of hydrogen go through fusion and become one atom of helium.

**magnetic field** (mag-NET-ik FEELD) A magnetic field is an area around an object where that object's magnetism affects other things. The sun's magnetic field affects the sun's hot gases.

**mass** (MASS) Mass is a measure of how much matter is in an object. The sun makes up most of the mass in the solar system.

**orbits** (OR-bits) An object orbits the sun when it travels in a round path around the sun. Earth orbits the sun.

**probes** (PROHBZ) Probes are spacecraft that fly without people inside. Some probes learn more about the sun.

**satellites** (SAT-uh-lites) Satellites are spacecraft that orbit a larger object in space. Many satellites orbit Earth.

**solar system** (SOH-ler SIS-tum) The solar system includes the sun and planets. The sun is at the center of the solar system.

# TO LEARN MORE

## IN THE LIBRARY

Bell, Samantha S. *Build a Solar Cooker*.
Mankato, MN: The Child's World, 2017.

Ponka, Katherine. *Math on the Sun*. New York, NY:
Gareth Stevens Publishing, 2017.

Rathburn, Betsy. *The Sun*. Minneapolis, MN:
Bellwether Media, 2019.

## ON THE WEB

Visit our website for links about the sun:
**childsworld.com/links**

*Note to Parents, Teachers, and Librarians: We routinely verify
our Web links to make sure they are safe and active sites.
So encourage your readers to check them out!*

# INDEX